SURFING
SOUTH WEST

Dave Hunter

Tor Mark Press

About the author

Dave Hunter lives and surfs in Newquay. In 1986 he was runner up in the kneeboard division of the English National Surfing Championships.

Published by Tor Mark Press, Islington Wharf,
Penryn, Cornwall TR10 8AT

First published 1989
© 1989 Tor Mark Press

ISBN 0-85025-302-0

Cover photograph by Sue Ciastula of Vitamin Sea Surfboards
Drawings by Delta Graphics, Falmouth

Printed by Swannack Brown & Co Ltd, Hull

What is surfing?

The essence of surfing is getting away from it all. Forget the 'surfer look' or the 'surfer sound'; what counts is what happens in the water. Beneath the trends and the fashion and the lifestyle is the simple act of riding a wave.

I've been surfing for many years and I'm still learning about the waves and my reaction to them. It's a process that never stops.

You can't talk about surfing from the beach because only the person on the board knows what it's all about. I hope this guide will help you gain in experience and find beaches to surf and enjoy.

It is organised in easy-to-find sections ranging from Starting out to Surf safety. The beach guide lists eight popular surfing locations, most with several beaches so about 20 beaches in all. At the back is a glossary of 150 surfing terms. Words in the glossary are set in italics the first time they appear in the text.

Enjoy your surfing!

Starting out: your first board and wetsuit

The first thing you need is a board that is right for *you*. When choosing a board, consider

 your body weight
 your height
 your general level of fitness
 your goal in surfing

For instance a thirteen year old weighing 100 1b and with the opportunity to surf regularly would start out on a 5'10" or 6' board.

The main consideration when choosing should be the overall width of the board. The wider the board the more stable it will be to start learning on. On the other hand, if the board is too large or too buoyant, it will feel cumbersome and difficult to control. Size and buoyancy are the starting points. Find your weight and this table will give you a rough idea of what to look for as your first board.

your weight	board length	board width
100-110lb	6'0"	20"
110-120	6'2"	20"
120-130	6'4"	20.5"
130-140	6'6"	20.5"
140-150	6'8"	20.5"
150-170	6'10"	21"
170-180	7'0"	21"
Over 180lb	7'0"	22"

Start by looking for a board that has a full *plan-shape*, and which maintains its width in the *nose* and *tail* areas. If you are starting out, it's a good idea to stay away from current fads or vogues in surf design, especially if the width of the board you are looking at tapers quickly from the centre to

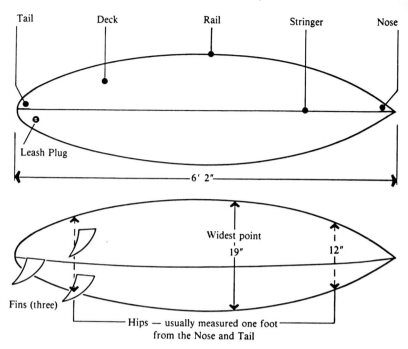

Board viewed from top

Tail   Deck   Rail   Stringer   Nose

Leash Plug

6' 2"

Widest point
19"   12"

Fins (three)

Hips — usually measured one foot
from the Nose and Tail

Board viewed from bottom

*Surfboards are traditionally measured by five dimensions: length — widest point —
both hip measurements (nose then tail) — general cross-sectional thickness. This
typical 'Thruster' surfboard might be 6'2" × 19" × 12" × 12" × 2.5".*

the nose and tail. The *rails* should be soft and rounded; if
you can feel a distinct hard edge where the rail line meets
the bottom of the board, leave this board to the experienced
surfer. Soft rails make the board stable and easier to
control. It's very appealing to buy your first board because
it looks good or because it looks like the ones in the surfing
magazines . . . but don't! I mean, who would learn to drive
in a Ferrari?

Don't be afraid to shop around. Check all the surfshops and
compare prices, ask questions and take your time.

Once you've decided to make your investment in a board,
you'll have to consider whether you want to buy a new one
or a secondhand one. If you don't have much money, a
secondhand board is a much safer investment. I think it's

far safer to buy your first board from an established surfshop because in the long run you'll get a better deal. Surfshops, like any other business, are out to make lasting customers; if you enjoy the first board you bought there, quite probably you'll go there first when you want to buy your next board. Also, a surfshop has experienced staff who can advise and answer any questions you might have.

Don't feel uncomfortable about asking questions on various board designs or surfing techniques. If a shop is in any way creditable, the staff are there to help you. All surfers have to start somewhere — we were all *gremmies* once. If in doubt, ask!

If you do decide to buy a secondhand board, treat it like buying a used car — it might be cheap but can you restore it and is it worth what you're paying? Unless you possess the necessary skills, stay away from restoration work with your first board. Obvious signs of a damaged board include unrepaired *dings*, yellow or brown patches of foam discolouration visible through the surface, fibreglass lifting up from the foam, and — as with an old car — a general sense of having been rather too well used and abused!

Once you find a board you really like, the first thing to do is to run your hands along the rails. Feel for any dings; press them firmly with your thumbs and if they are very soft and give easily, pass up that board as it will probably need expensive repair work. Take a close look at the *fin* or fins, check their condition and see if they are still fixed solidly to the bottom of the board. If there are any cracks where the fin meets the bottom surface, think again! If the board has *fin boxes*, check for any looseness in the fins and see if the box still fits properly.

All these problems are relative, particularly to the price the seller expects! If in doubt, haggle or ask for a quote to make the damage good.

You may consider buying a *pop-out* or moulded surfboard. The problem here is the very nature of the product. What you will be buying is a fixed size board, usually around 7'0" by 22". There are clear limitations to this type of board and I think it's better to aim for something as close as possible to your ideal requirements, albeit secondhand. If you really only intend to surf for recreation for a fortnight a year, then a pop-out may be ideal for you.

The next essential is a *wetsuit*. Any ideas you may have of surfing Hawaii-style in a pair of *baggies* will be rapidly dispelled when you hit the cold Atlantic — even in August! Buying a wetsuit is rather different from finding a suitable board.

Ideally a wetsuit should be a custom fit, because it works by trapping between the rubber and your skin a layer of water which is then heated by your own body temperature. Clearly, an ill-fitting wetsuit is about as useful as a cumbersome surfboard. There are many specialist wetsuit manufacturers and, as with surfshops, they are qualified to advise on an appropriate suit.

When you are starting out, if you have limited funds it is better to spend more money on a new wetsuit than on a new board. After all, when you are learning you are going to spend more time in the water than out of it! If you do decide to buy a secondhand wetsuit there are obvious considerations. It should be as good a fit as possible: it should fit where it touches without being too tight or constricting your movements. Before you buy any suit, turn it inside out and check the stitching for signs of wear or snagging. Take a close look at the knees and elbows to see if they show signs of extra wear and tear. Pay particular attention to the zip: it can be quite a cold shock if it breaks while you are surfing!

Wetsuits and pop-out surfboards can be hired by the day or week from most surfshops or at the larger municipal beaches.

Waves and beaches

The starting point of surfing is waves, but the starting point of waves is the wind. Without wind the sea would remain flat and there would be no surf. Sometimes local coastal winds can create waves, a so-called *wind swell*, but it is storms occurring hundreds or even thousands of miles out to sea which create the true ocean swell that will break on the coastline as consistent surf.

As the wind blows across the surface of the sea it creates ripples; if the wind is strong and lasts long enough, these ripples will grow into a *swell* that travels in the same direction as the wind itself. This swell will in theory travel, increasing or decreasing, until it reaches land perhaps a thousand miles later. When you see a swell out to sea, it looks as though the water is moving sideways. This is deceptive, because it isn't. A wave is like a pulse which moves through the water: the water itself does not start to move forward until the wave breaks.

A wave begins to break when it reaches shallow water. As it approaches the shoreline it begins to build up to a *peak*. The *face* of the wave becomes steeper as the water at its base becomes shallower and then it begins to break. The top or *lip* of the wave will start to crumple over causing the white water foam effect which drives in towards the shore.

The shape of the breaking wave is determined by the shape of the ocean floor. If the bottom has a gradual slope, as is often the case with sandy *beach breaks*, the wave will tend to break gently from the top. If the water shallows suddenly, or there is a reef on the ocean floor, the wave is more likely to rear up suddenly and break in a more defined curl.

If you compare both types of breaking wave, say at Towan Beach in Newquay and Porthleven in south Cornwall, the difference is startling.

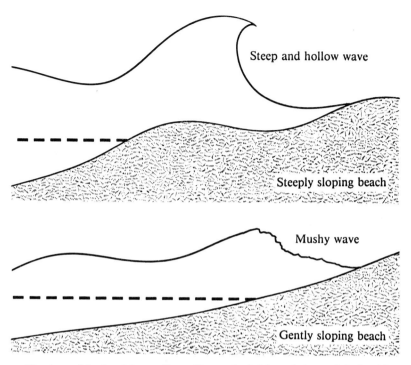

The slope of the beach has a direct effect on the height and shape of the breaking wave.

The size of a wave has always been in the eye of the beholder, and you will often get a variety of estimations. There are two main ways of estimating the height — from the front or the back as shown in the diagram.

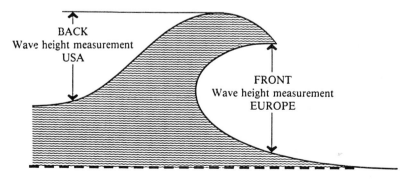

Surfers and beaches

Surfers' reputations depend on each other. When you arrive at a beach new to you, you will be judged on the actions of those who were there last week. It can take a few misplaced seconds to ruin many months of hard cooperation with local councils and beach owners. Follow these simple rules and make everyone's stay a pleasant one.

- Don't try to dodge car park fees; one car with boards on top will brand all those which follow it.

- Think about your own granny when getting changed! Would she really like you showing your credentials to all and sundry?

- Watch where you leave your boards lying around. Car insurance does not cover running over 'parked' surfboards, especially in a private car park. I should know — it happened to me once at Fistral!

- The same applies to your wetsuit. Watch out, there are many light fingers about and on a crowded beach your gear can be history in seconds.

- Don't litter, particularly those ubiquitous wax wrappers!

- Close all gates behind you.

- Respect pedestrians. With a board under your arm you are taking up at least three times the amount of car park or footpath that they are. Carry your board with its fins facing inwards, and take care when suddenly turning round. Watch out for small children.

- Remember, a smile and a joke can be worth a thousand misplaced words.

Surf safety

The Atlantic Ocean is one of the world's largest sources of energy. Many of the waves hitting the Cornish coast have travelled thousands of miles from the mid Atlantic: they are very powerful and potentially very dangerous. You must always respect the power of the ocean — it will not discriminate in the way it treats you! Here are a few fundamental tips.

● When you arrive at the beach, always check with the lifeguards whether there are any surfing or bathing restrictions. There will almost certainly be a council notice on larger beaches.

● Never enter the surf directly after a meal or if you have been drinking. A combination of hot summer sun, warm beer and cold Atlantic can quickly lead to trouble and can quite easily be fatal.

Spot the idiots!

- Always check the prevailing wind conditions and estimate the position of the tide. You can buy a tide-table at most newsagents.

- Take real care with *rip currents*. You can recognise them by the unusual rippling effect on the water's surface, and usually the surf will stop breaking in the area of a rip. If you are caught in one, don't panic and don't try to paddle against it. You must paddle at right angles to its flow until you are out of it; rip currents are usually no more than twenty feet wide.

- When surfing, stay away from rocks and cliff edges.

- If you do get into difficulties, don't panic. Try to remain calm. By raising one arm vertically in the air you will alert the lifeguard to your difficulty — this is an internationally recognised surf-lifesaving action.

- Never surf alone.

- Do not surf in a swimming area.

- In the early stages do not go too far out to sea and always try to be aware of your position in relation to the shoreline. Look for a significant landmark or building: it will mean you will not drift.

- Never leave your surfboard. It will keep you afloat and if you remain in the surf zone you will be pushed towards the beach.

This sounds like a long and frightening list. It need not be if you are sensible and do not exceed your limitations.

First steps with your board

The first thing you need to do with your new board is to wax the deck. Blocks of *wax* in a variety of shapes, perfumes and prices can be obtained at all surfshops. Lay your board fins down on the sand and, using the edge of the block of wax, rub the deck across with small circular movements until you gradually build up a semi-sticky coating. You should try to do this before each surf session so that the wax gradually builds up on the surface of your board. Without a good coating of wax you won't get very far. Remember to extend your covering right to the edge of the rails; this will become important when you first try to stand up.

Next, check the surf. Spend a few minutes looking at it very closely. Experienced surfers do this while they are getting changed; it will become second nature to you but in the early stages it's a good idea to make it a conscious effort. Try to spot where the waves are actually breaking. Is it possible to work out which part of the beach has more surf? Where are the majority of other surfers heading towards? Are there any obvious hazards visible — submerged rocks or young swimmers on the shoreline? Before you actually enter the water, it is important to check with the lifeguard where the surfing area on that particular beach actually is. Believe me, nothing will dampen your enthusiasm more than someone bawling at you from fifty yards away with a megaphone.

Final check: wetsuit zip fully fastened, board fully waxed? Time to put on the *leash*; you'll probably find it most comfortable on your right ankle; most leashes fasten by a velcro closure and are easy to lock tight.

When you are at the water's edge, and certainly by the time you are knee deep, you'll appreciate how powerful the

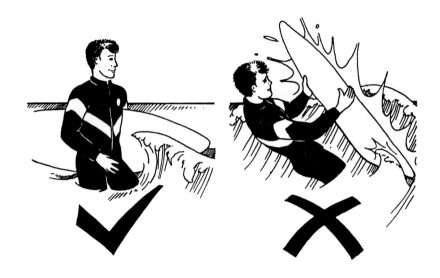

Entering the water. Always hold the board to the side of your body; don't put it between you and the sea or the oncoming wave will soon knock you over!

waves and surf really are. It's at this point that you should stop for a second and check that you are entering the water at the right place. Make sure that the waves are small — less than three feet — and breaking gently. Even the smallest wave will have the power to push you forward without knocking you around too much.

Make sure the board is pointing out to sea. The less surface area that gets hit by a wave, the less chance there is that you will be knocked around by it.

Don't even think about *paddling out* right into the *line-up*. The first thing you want to do is to get used to the feel of your board in the water — it's quite different when it's floating. Notice how the nose of the board clearly rises above the surface. Try to remember that angle, because when you do begin to paddle and *take off*, that's the angle you must try to keep the board at.

Wade out to about waist depth, keeping always seaward of your board. If you don't, an incoming wave will soon push you and your board over! If a wave is approaching which has already broken, you can float your board over the top of it by grasping hold of both rails, one hand across the deck, at about the mid point of the board's length. As the wave hits you, gently push down the tail and the nose will rise further and begin to plane over the white water. Obviously the success of this depends on your own forward momentum — lean forwards lightly into the wave at the same time. You will see other surfers doing this — it almost looks as though they are pushing the bottom side of their boards at the incoming waves.

When you feel comfortable in the water, you've got used to the weight of your board, you're beginning to appreciate your wetsuit and you've had a good look around your immediate sea area and there's nothing in your way — you are ready to start.

Lie prone on the deck of your board, not too far up because the nose will dip under, not too far back because then you will push too much water. After you have rolled off a few times, in a very undignified manner, you will find the right prone position in relation to your own weight and the length of the board. If you remember what it looked like floating, that is what it should still look like even with you on it. Make a mental note of your position for future occasions.

You are now ready to try to catch your first wave, but before you do, a warning note on how to fall off properly! It is not always possible to do it correctly but the aim is to fall away from your board and into the back of the wave. This will allow your board to be carried away from you, so don't worry if you feel a slight tug on the surf-leash. When you come to the surface, always emerge with your hands over your head. It's natural, especially when you are learning, to want to clear yourself from the water as soon as possible, but remember, when you fell off you had no idea where the board went. Boards have an annoying habit of floating exactly where you are going to surface or even remaining in mid-air waiting for you! Many experienced surfers lift their heads very slowly after a *wipeout*.

Try to catch a smallish wave to begin with. It does not matter if it has already broken. Point your board straight towards the beach and as the wave approaches start paddling. The precise moment to start paddling is hard to define. You should certainly start when the wave is a couple of yards away from you, and you should paddle aggressively as you feel the wave start to lift your board. A common mistake is to stop paddling too early — don't, make sure you have really *caught the wave*. You will know because your forward speed will increase dramatically.

As soon as possible, place your hands on the deck of the board approximately under your chest area, fingertips on the edge of the rail line. Imagine you are going to do a press-up in the gym, only complete the action and stand up as soon as possible. Speed is of the essence. Don't try to clamber up or place one knee on the deck first. The take-off is one of the most difficult things to master; it's worth persevering with and getting it right from the word go. Ideally it should be a single fluid manoeuvre and when you are starting it will certainly tell you something about your sense of balance!

There is no right or wrong way about which foot goes forward. Most surfers lead with their left foot, but many lead with the right or *goofy foot*. Go with whichever feels comfortable, but if you lead with your right you may want the leash on your left ankle so that you don't tread on it.

The take-off needs a lot of practice. You can easily improve your technique by practising on the beach a few times. The first time you try it on the water it will probably feel very unstable, and the chances are you will have your feet too close together. Try widening your stance to about two feet,

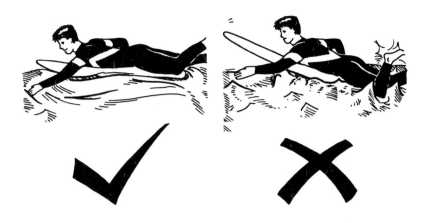

Correct paddling position. The nose of your board should just break the surface of the water; you will then plane. Trim forward when you start to paddle — too far back and the tail will sink, the nose will push water and progress will be slow.

Standing position once you have taken off. Balance is crucial; try to stand approximately either side of the board's centre point. If you stand too far back on the tail, the nose will lift and you will fall off! If you stand too near the nose it will dip and you will fall forward. Balance is everything!

17

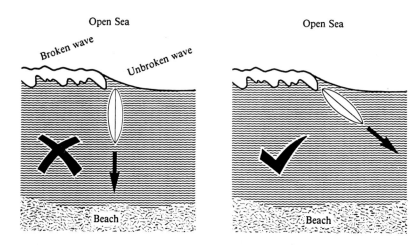

Trimming the board for the best possible ride. Try to surf as close to the wave face as possible; you should try to ride almost parallel to the unbroken wave face itself.

knees slightly bent to help you balance, and your head over your leading foot. This should lead to greater stability. Spend as much time as possible mastering this early technique: it will pay dividends in the long run.

Now that you are up and riding, it is time to consider what is actually happening. Don't try to look round to see if your mates are watching or you will probably fall off! Try to look at a spot about a yard ahead of the nose. That way you can keep an eye on the wave and you get a sense of the relative speed of wave and board.

A word of warning: always keep well clear of other surfers who are already riding and never take off on a wave if you even appear to be lined up with another surfer paddling out, or with a bather. Any sort of surf collision, however apparently minor, can be serious and expensive.

All you need now is lots of practice . . . .

Some good surfing beaches

I have selected these beaches on the grounds that they have good parking and easy access, that they are lifeguard patrolled during the summer season and have proved popular with novices and experienced surfers alike. But always remember 'popular' does not necessarily always mean 'safe'; surf conditions can change dramatically with each tide and two foot waves can become six foot waves in a matter of hours! Always seek local advice and consult the lifeguards.

Saunton Sands, North Devon

Saunton Sands is a massive, sweeping beach break which can work at all stages of the tide. It is a west-facing beach which is generally sheltered from the strong northerly cross winds by Croyde Point to the north.

In actual fact the beach area is so large that it has several beach breaks that tend to change position with the tides. The beach is almost two miles long and long rides are possible on gently breaking, slow moving waves so it is an ideal beach for the novice and very popular in the summer months. At low tide it is almost half a mile wide, so there is plenty of space for everybody. Saunton is also ideal for spectators who, especially as the tide advances, can view the surf from the cliff roadside to the immediate north of the beach. You can park on the road and walk down the grassy slope to the beach or use the large beach-side car park.

The true beauty of the area is that there are plenty of good quality surfing beaches quite close together: to the north is *Croyde*, a fast-breaking experts' beach, further north is *Putsborough* and finally *Woolacombe*, both of which are long sand beaches.

Bude

Summerleaze, north of the river mouth, produces a reliable right hand breaking wave that works on biggish swells. It can appear to be a complex situation because of the position of the harbour wall and the river on the south side can completely flatten out a weak swell. There can be a patch of sandbar breaks working off the swimming pool area of this beach; as the tide rises you can take off from the rocks beside the pool. This area can appear sheltered when Crooklets Beach is closed out.

Crooklets Beach, immediately to the north of the swimming pool area, is the other main town surfing area. It is another break that is dependent upon shifting sandbanks and can work well at low or high tide. Take care with the backwash off the rocks at high tide. This beach is really best in small and glassy conditions: it can easily start to close out.

Both beaches face west. There is adequate local parking, although it can easily get crowded at the height of the summer season.

Newquay

There are four main beaches in Newquay Bay — the 'Bay Area' — and at low tide they form one large sweeping expanse of golden sand. The whole of the Bay Area works best on a south-westerly wind, which is common even in summer. The southern part of the bay is much more sheltered by cliffs and headlands than the northern end.

The most northerly beach and therefore most exposed is *Lusty Glaze* which is privately owned and does sometimes restrict surfing in the summer depending on the number of swimmers and the density of the crowds. There is a longish walk down a flight of steps, with café facilities and toilets. Lusty Glaze works best at low to half tide on an incoming swell.

The next beach is *Tolcarne* and again there is a steep flight of steps, although in winter it is just possible to drive down. This too is privately owned, but because of its larger size, especially at low water, there are no surfing restrictions. This larger beach will work well at all stages of the tide, though a rising tide is preferable. As with the whole Bay Area, the sandy bottom is very variable depending on local storms and swell patterns. You will find you can check surfing conditions on this beach and its southern neighbour from the viewing platform on the intervening cliff top.

Great Western Beach is smack in the centre of the town, at the bottom of a long sweeping roadway which leads down from the cliff top. There are parking restrictions throughout Newquay during the summer, but from September to May there is limited parking for about a dozen cars — though watch out for broken glass.

This beach is probably the most popular in Newquay and it is rideable at all stages of the tide, although it is best from half to three-quarter on an incoming tide. At high tide there is very little sand remaining and you must take care to look out for the large submerged rock in the centre of the high water mark. If you enjoy surfing with a crowd of people at all times of the year, this is the place to come.

The southernmost beach in the Bay Area is *Towan Beach*, which is sheltered by the harbour and the headland. There is plenty of unrestricted winter parking and you can get a good view of the surf from the promenade area near the Cosy Nook Theatre. Like Great Western Beach, this works best on a south-westerly wind, but because it is so sheltered it tends to work in virtually all wind situations. If everywhere else in town is closed out, there is usually some shelter at Towan, but you will find every other surfer has had the same idea. Expect large crowds even in winter.

Towan works best at half to three-quarters tide; at high tide you can easily get a potentially dangerous backwash off the promenade wall. At low tide you sometimes get a really quality left hand breaking wave off the harbour wall but this is a rare event requiring a perfect combination of wind, swell and sea-bottom contour. At present there are daytime (9am to 6pm) restrictions on surfing at Towan from April to September. If in doubt, ask the local lifeguard.

Around the headland, on the other side of Newquay, is the legendary *Fistral Beach*, home of international surfing competitions and site of the 1986 World Amateur Surfing Championships. This is a west facing beach which can produce a world class beachbreak wave. Fistral generally works best at low tide and, as with other Cornish beaches, it all still depends on the bottom contour of the ocean floor. It is such a large and exposed beach that it easily picks up ocean swell, with the result that the sand bottom is always changing. Fairly long rides are possible, and the shape of the surf will improve with an increasing swell. In winter it is not uncommon to ride three or four days together of six to eight foot swell.

The main beach is known as *North Fistral*, with plenty of parking, a large beach café and public toilets. This main beach area works best on a southerly wind and at low tide can produce, given the right sandbar conditions, a quality tubing wave. It is predominantly a right breaking wave and care should be taken about surfing towards the left — towards Little Fistral — as high water approaches because you will be heading into an area of many submerged rocks and difficult rip currents. At high tide there can be a very powerful shorebreak, because the beach can shelve very steeply indeed. If you enter the water at high tide, you must be prepared for a hard paddle into the line-up.

South Fistral is the southern end of the main beach and can be reached by road along the Pentire headland. You can park at the roadside and the beach area is at the foot of the cliffside steps. This is a high tide location, especially if North Fistral is cross shore, when the headland offers real protection. Whereas the north end offers largely right hand breaking waves, the southern end offers mainly left hand. With a good swell running you can have really long rides but the take-off area can easily become very crowded. If the swell is particularly large it is possible but not advisable to enter the water from the small cliffs halfway along the headland, avoiding an arduous paddle out. I don't recommend this because it can give you a false sense of security. If the broken waves are too powerful for you to paddle straight out, then you shouldn't be in the water!

The whole of Fistral can become very crowded in the summer, especially in August when the international professional championships are held. Expect large crowds and act accordingly — take care!

Perranporth

This extensive beach can be divided into three main surfing areas. At the northern extreme is *Penhale Corner*, a delightful sandy beach surrounded by toweringly high cliffs and backed by very steep sand dunes. It is almost secluded, so much so that it is favoured by naturists, and involves a long walk across and down the sand dunes from the holiday camp at the top of the cliffs. I don't think I have ever walked back up the dunes by the same route I had travelled down, such is the extent of the dunes.

The whole of Perranporth beach is west facing and is about a mile and a half long. The Penhale Corner area works best on a southerly wind and can produce some of the longest rides in Cornwall. When it is working and the sand bottom is just right it is an almost perfect wave which can never become too crowded because there can often be four or five separate peaks working within the same surfing area. You can park at the top of the dunes but take care you don't get stuck in the soft sand; it can and does happen quite frequently.

The mid-section of the beach is known as *Penhale Sands*; if you decide to walk up to the beach at low water from Perranporth, take extreme care. The OS map refers to quicksand and they are not kidding! This is the most open part of the beach and as such can easily suffer from extremes of wind. You can get good rights and lefts off the sandy bottom but be ready for a long and hard paddle out if a big swell is running. This is an area of shifting beach breaks whose position can change with the tide. If the conditions are really good, it can be worth the long walk from the main town area. If you don't fancy the walk and prefer to park in Perranporth itself, then you can surf off the area fronted by the life-saving hut.

The southern section of the beach is called *Droskyn* and it can produce some sizeable left hand breaking waves towards the mouth of the river Perran by Chapel Rock. At high tide take care to avoid the many submerged rocks.

This whole beach area can produce some quality waves, but it also has some of the strongest rip currents in Cornwall. It is no place for weak swimmers. If in doubt, seek local advice from the surfshops or council lifeguard. Although it is a massive beach area, the holiday-makers do tend to congregate in crowds in the main town area of the beach.

Sennen Cove

This is the beach which forms the southern end of Whitesand Bay and is the most south-westerly surfing beach in the UK. As such it has the greatest potential for picking up Atlantic swells. There is a large beach car park at the bottom of the steep hill which leads into the village of Sennen. The main surfing area is in front and to the right of the beach café. The beach faces north-west and is best on a southerly wind. It can suffer from shifting sandbanks although on the whole it is a very reliable surf break offering a variety of peaks.

If one area of the beach is crowded, just walk northwards and try somewhere else. At the northerly end is Aire Point and this beach area is known as *Gwenver Beach*; it's a mile or so along the coastal footpath from the cove car park, or you can drive back up the hill and along the road to Escalls. It really is worth the walk, because even if you drive you will still have quite a walk down the grassy cliff. If the surf is three feet in the cove, it may well be five feet at Gwenver.

Praa Sands

A sandy south-west facing beach which breaks fairly regularly if a good swell is running into a strong northerly wind. It is a beach break which works best on a rising tide. At high tide it can start to close out very easily. There is parking opposite the pub at the beach side, and public conveniences. Of all the south coast beaches west of the Lizard, this is the most reliable for surf in winter; in summer it can be very fickle.

Caerhays and Pentewan

The south coast west of the Lizard has few regular surfing beaches, largely because it faces the wrong way for the dominant swell patterns and is sheltered by the Lizard peninsula. I have selected two which are, in some small way, reasonably consistent but they are really only winter surf breaks. Be warned: both these beaches can be a hit or miss affair, perhaps producing rideable surf on only one side of the tide.

In Veryan Bay there is a small pebbly beach at *Caerhays* which faces due south and will work if a strong swell is met by a northerly wind. It can work from low to high tide, depending on the strength of the swell.

Pentewan, in Mevagissey Bay, is a long sandy beach facing south-east. Given a good strong swell and a south-westerly wind, you may find rideable surf in the centre or south end. It works from low to threequarter tide; at high tide it can shelve too steeply and close.

Bantham

This south-west facing beach is easily the most reliable on the south coast of Devon. It is a river mouth break; the river Avon runs to the west of the beach and the east side is bounded by rocks. The beach is backed by generous sand dunes, behind which you can usually park pretty close to the sea. It works at all stages of the tide, but you must take care when the dropping tide combines with the river current. It is predominantly a winter break, which can easily throw up a surprise in summer. It is definitely worth a try if you are in the Plymouth/South Devon area, as also are *Wembury* and *Salcombe*.

Clearly there are other breaks along this coast, as indeed there are many I have not mentioned along the north coast. All you need is luck and the right conditions of wind and wave and you will find them. Part of the fun is discovery. Good luck!

Glossary

Surfing, like all sports, has its own special vocabulary, which constantly changes. Some of the following terms are no longer in general use — but they could reappear at any time!

A.S.P.: Association of Surfing Professionals — governing body of international professional surfing contests

astrodeck: product name for a grip pad adhering to the rear of a surfboard deck, and giving increased traction during turns

backhand surfing: riding a wave with the surfer's own back facing the wave

back off: a wave that appears to begin to break but does not and becomes whole again

baggies: loose fitting shorts

balsa wood: soft, porous wood used for surfboard construction in the 1930s

bank: a section of beach that rises steeply, which can affect the quality of surf passing over it

beach break: a surf break forming on a sand bottomed beach

beating sections: surfing backwards or forwards in order to avoid the closing white water at the top of the breaking wave

belly board: short narrow marine-plywood board, in use since the 1930s; a short board used for prone riding in already broken surf

blank: highly compressed foam, made in a mould, from which custom surfboards are shaped; the core of a surfboard

blown out: when strong winds make the waves unrideable; a choppy windblown sea

body surfing: catching a wave with your body, planing forward

Boogie board: short plastic surfboard, similar to a belly board, usually ridden prone

bottom turn: turning on a surfboard at the bottom the wave's face

break: action of a wave as the top spills forward down its face *or* the area of sea where the waves are breaking and becoming rideable

B.S.A.: British Surfing Association, Burrows Chambers, East Burrows Road, Swansea SA1 1RF

catch the wave: to begin to ride the wave

channel: area of deeper water where the waves do not break, often used by surfers as an access route to the breaking surf; may be dangerous, as rip currents can be found in deeper water

clean-up: a set of larger waves which break further out, wiping out the surfers waiting to take off

climbing and dropping: surfing up and down the face of a wave

close-out: occurs when a heavy swell breaks along the entire length of a beach, making surfing impossible

covered up: surfing in the tube, when the face of the wave completely covers the surfer in a hollow fashion

crest: top of the wave that is beginning to spill over

critical: a wave reaches the critical stage when it is almost vertical and is about to break

curl: the part of a wave which loops over to form a curl as it breaks, usually the top section of a hollow wave

custom board: a surfboard made to the individual requirements of the surfer

cut back: to make a 180° turn while surfing, in order to ride back over a section of the wave face

decal: paper or plastic labels used to display trade names of surfboard manufacturers

deck: the part of the board you stand on

ding: damage to a surfboard

drop in: taking off in front of another surfer, so ruining their ride — to be avoided at all costs

dumping surf: a wave that breaks suddenly, so ruining a ride (similar to closing out)
duck diving: pushing the nose of your surfboard under the water as a breaking wave approaches, in order to avoid being pushed towards the shore by semi-submerging your board and yourself

emmets: old Cornish word for ants, now used to describe tourists

face: the smooth unbroken part of a wave
fin: the fin or fins serve the same function as the keel of a yacht
fin box: countersunk narrow box, approximately 7″ by 1″, glassed into the bottom of a surfboard, enabling the fin to be adjusted by a tensioned screw
foam: the inner core material of a board, see *blank*

glassing: laminating fibreglass cloth onto the shaped blank
glassy: used to describe perfect surfing waves, undisturbed by adverse wind conditions
goofy foot: surfer who rides with his right foot forward
gremmie: novice surfer, especially a youngster
ground swell: swell which has travelled a long way from where it was formed
gun: longer than average surfboard designed for big waves

hang five: to place five toes over the nose of the surfboard while riding
hang ten: as above, but with ten toes
head dip: to dip your head in the wave while riding the board
hollow: concave face of the wave
hot dog surfing: surfing quickly, using maximum manoeuvres

inside break: waves closest to the shore
inside: to ride close to the wave face

kick out: to turn sharply up the face of the wave as a means of ending the ride
kneeboard: short surfboard used for riding on one's knees

kook: slang term for a novice surfer, see *gremmie*

leash: safety line, usually made of stressed nylon rope encased in rubber, attached to a surfer's ankle and to the deck of the board

leash plug: plastic cup with a bar across, glassed and countersunk into the deck of a surfboard; a leash is then tied across the barred plug

left/right: direction in which a wave breaks or surfer travels *as seen when facing the shore*

line up: point where the waves are beginning to break and surfers are waiting to catch a wave

lip: leading edge of the curl of a breaking wave

locked in: when the tail of the board is held by the wave; in straight line surfing, the fastest part of the ride

mal: shortened form of malibu, used to describe a surfboard over eight feet long designed for general surfing, see *gun*

Malibu: Californian beach which gave its name to the first foam boards, which were made in Malibu

mat: rubber Lilo-type float; can be used for belly surfing

mushy: term used to describe a wave that breaks and dies out quickly, leading to a short ride

natural foot: surfer who rides with his left foot forward

neap tide: tide in which the high and low water levels are very close together

nose: the pointed front of a surfboard

nose ride: to stand near the front of the board while surfing

outside: the area of sea beyond where the waves are breaking

out the back: to be out to sea, beyond where the waves are breaking

over the falls: when a surfer is pitched forward and falls with the breaking white water

paddling out: lying prone on the deck, using your hands to paddle out to the line up

peak: the starting point of a wave, where it begins to break

pearl: to allow the nose of a surfboard to dig under the water surface, thereby throwing the surfer off
pick up: area where the surfer first catches the wave
pintail: a surfboard with a pointed tail
plan shape: outline of a surfboard seen from above
point surf: surf breaking off a point of coastline
pop-out: board mass-produced from a mould and not needing hand shaping, used by most surfboard hire firms

quad: four finned surfboard

radical: extreme
rails: the edges of a surfboard
rail saver: short length of canvas-type fabric, attached between the leash and the surfboard, which lessens the tension on the deck during a wipeout and prevents the leash 'cheese-wiring' the deck
reef break: surf forming and breaking over a submerged rock or coral reef
re-entry: surfing up the face of a wave and then turning back onto the soup
resin: liquid adhesive used in binding glassfibre cloth to the shaped blank
rip: a current which drains back into the sea; some rip currents travel at a speed of several knots and are therefore very dangerous
rocker: amount of lateral curve or lift in a surfboard nose or tail

section: part of a wave
set: series of waves following rapidly one after another
shaper: occupational name of someone who carves surfboards
shore break: surf which breaks on or close to the shoreline
shoulder: that part of the wave closest to the curl
single fin: board with one central fin
skeg: slang term for a surfboard fin
slide: riding along the face of the wave in a straight line
slot: the fastest part of the wave, close to the curl
soup: broken white water caused when the wave collapses

spin out: losing control of a ride because the fin of the surfboard has broken free of the wave face

spring tide: tide in which the high and low water levels are very far apart

stall: to stand towards the tail of a surfboard to slow it down

stoked: excited

stringer: narrow strip of wood running down the centre of a surfboard, used to give extra strength

surfer: person encased in black rubber, usually cold and frequently dripping — but never complaining!

swell: series of waves

switchfoot: surfer who can change leading foot while surfing

tail: rear of a surfboard

take-off: the start of a ride

take-off zone: area where most surfers start their rides

thruster: board with three fins, two forward of a single rear fin

trimming: positioning of a surfer on a wave

trough: calm space of sea between waves

tube: hollow space created when a wave crest peels over

turning: changing direction on a surfboard

twin fin: surfboard with two fins

undertow: current of water travelling below the surface

wall: the face of a wave

wax: a block of wax, paraffin based, rubbed on to prevent slipping; many varieties available

wedge: wave that is formed when one wave hits another wave coming in a different direction

wetsuit: suit of neoprene rubber, worn as a protection against the cold

wind swell: waves created solely by the wind

wipeout: falling off a surfboard

woody: originally a wood panelled station waggon; usually refers to any form of camper van transportation